THE GREAT LITTLE BOOK OF SAUCES

get saucy

THE GREAT LITTLE BOOK OF SAUCES

get saucy

Emma Summer

southwater

This edition is published by Southwater
Southwater is an imprint of Anness Publishing Ltd
Hermes House, 88–89 Blackfriars Road, London SE1
8HA; tel. 020 7401 2077; fax 020 7633 9499
www.southwaterbooks.com; info@anness.com
© Anness Publishing Ltd 1997, 2002

Published in the USA by Southwater, Anness Publishing
Inc., 27 West 20th Street, New York, NY 10011;
fax 212 807 6813

This edition distributed in the UK by The Manning
Partnership Ltd, ; tel. 01225 478 444; fax 01225 478
440; sales@manning-partnership.co.uk
This edition distributed in the USA by National Book
Network; tel. 301 459 3366; fax 301 459 1705;
www.nbnbooks.com
This edition distributed in Canada by General Publishing;
tel. 416 445 3333; fax 416 445 5991; www.genpub.com
This edition distributed in Australia by Pan Macmillan
Australia; tel. 1300 135 113; fax 1300 135 103;
email customer.service@macmillan.com.au
This edition distributed in New Zealand by The Five Mile
Press (NZ) Ltd; tel. (09) 444 4144; fax (09) 444 4518;
fivemilenz@clear.net.nz

Publisher Joanna Lorenz
Managing Editor Linda Fraser
Editor Sarah Ainley
Copy Editor Jenni Fleetwood
Designers Patrick McLeavey & Jo Brewer
Illustrator Anna Koska
Photographers James Duncan
Recipes Nicola Diggins

Previously published as *Making Classic Sauces*
10 9 8 7 6 5 4 3 2 1

NOTES

For all recipes, quantities are given in both metric and
imperial measures and, where appropriate, measures are
also given in standard cups and spoons. Follow one set, but
not a mixture, because they are not interchangeable.
Standard spoon and cup measures are level.
1 tsp = 5ml, 1 tbsp = 15ml, 1 cup = 250ml/8fl oz
Australian standard tablespoons are 20ml. Australian
readers should use 3 tsp in place of 1 tbsp for measuring
small quantities of gelatine, cornflour, salt, etc.
Medium eggs are used unless otherwise stated.

Contents

Introduction

It may be that manners maketh the man but sauces add sweetness and savour to his meals. Even the simplest dishes, such as steamed cauliflower or boiled pasta, can be transformed by the addition of a creamy cheese sauce or a tasty tomato topping.

Meats are tenderised and given extra flavour when steeped in a spicy marinade. Salsas can be served solo, with a selection of dippers, or used to add piquancy to grills and barbecues.

A stock of sweet sauce recipes should be in every cook's repertoire. Silky smooth chocolate sauce turns a scoop of shop-bought ice cream into a tempting treat, especially if you add a sprinkling of toasted almonds and a couple of sponge fingers or other dessert biscuits. Home-made custard – or crème Anglaise, to give it its proper name – is truly delicious however you serve it, whether poured over fruit, served with a steamed pudding, or in a trifle or bavarois.

Sauces have, unfairly, got the reputation for being tricky. It is odd that something as innocuous as a white sauce can provoke such panic in the heart of a novice cook. Lumpy sauce jokes have a lot to answer for. In reality, making a white sauce could not be simpler. As long as you keep the heat low in the early stages, add the liquid gradually (it helps if you warm it first), and whisk vigorously all the time, you can't go far wrong. And if lumps do form, the sauce can almost certainly be saved if you take it off the heat and give it a jolly good beating.

It is also helpful to remember that

sauces based on a roux (the butter and flour mixture you begin with) can be made in advance and reheated. Just cover the surface closely with buttered grease-proof paper or clear film, to prevent the formation of a skin. When you are ready to serve, remove the covering and reheat the sauce slowly, whisking constantly.

Sauces thickened with egg, such as Hollandaise, can be a little more difficult. The enemy here is excessive heat, which will curdle the mixture. If this does happen, removing the pan from the heat and whisking in about 2 tablespoons of boiling water will often rescue the situation.

Salsas and other cold sauces are simplicity itself, and a boon to the busy cook. Most of them improve on keeping, so it is a positive advantage to make them ahead of time. An exception is guacamole, a cold avocado salsa that tends to discolour on standing. Even this will be fine for a short time if you cover the surface closely.

The quality of the ingredients is of prime importance when making sauces. Use the freshest vegetables and fruits and the best stock available (preferably home-made), take your time and remember to keep tasting. Recipes are invaluable, but not inviolate. Adding a whisper of wine, a sprinkling of herbs or a swirl of cream can make all the difference between a straightforward sauce and one that is absolutely sensational. Try it and see!

7

Ingredients

BUTTER

First choice for flavour, butter is used with flour as the basis of many classic sauces, although an oil-based roux is preferred by Cajun and Creole cooks.

CHEESE

Some of the world's finest sauces are flavoured with cheese, from the classic accompaniment for cauliflower to pasta's perfect partner, Gorgonzola & Walnut Sauce. Don't throw away those small pieces of cheese left on the cheeseboard after a dinner party. Mixed judiciously and stirred into a hot white or mushroom sauce, they can create some wonderful new taste sensations.

CHOCOLATE

Seductively smooth, chocolate makes a delicious dessert sauce. Melt it over a gentle heat, with cream, butter and sugar.

CREAM

Often stirred in at the end of cooking, cream can also be whipped before being folded in. Cream makes a useful decoration: drip double cream from a teaspoon to make small dots, then draw a cocktail stick gently through the dots to make them into heart shapes.

FRUIT

Both sweet and savoury sauces are made from fruit, with oranges a firm favourite alongside berry fruits of all kinds. Tomatoes make marvellous sauces, whether hot or cold.

HERBS

Classic herb-based sauces include mint, parsley, dill, basil and saffron, but herbs are also used for accent in almost all savoury sauces. If a bouquet garni is called for, tie together a bay leaf and a sprig each of thyme, marjoram and parsley.

OILS

Oil is used both for frying vegetables and as an emulsifier in many cold sauces, dips and marinades. Always use the specified type, as it will have been chosen to blend with the other ingredients. Extra-virgin olive oil, for instance, may have too dominant a flavour for some sauces.

STOCK

Many hot sauces depend for their flavour on a good quality stock. Make your own if you possibly can or use canned consommé. Stock cubes are a useful storecupboard stand-by, but tend to be rather salty.

VEGETABLES

A glance through this book will highlight the many vegetables that can be used for sauce-making. Onions and mushrooms feature frequently, with some of the finest sauces spotlighting a single vegetable, such as watercress. Salsas are made from chopped or puréed cold vegetables, often with spicy dressings.

WINE & LIQUEURS

Wine finds its way into many sauces, and is particularly useful in marinades. Liqueurs add extra flavour to several dessert sauces and often echo the main ingredient, as when Grand Marnier is stirred into an orange sauce.

9

Making Stock

BEEF STOCK

Also called brown stock, this is the basis for many richly flavoured sauces. Put 1kg/2¼lb raw beef shin or marrow bones in a roasting tin. Add 1 large carrot, quartered, 3 thickly sliced celery sticks and 1 onion (washed but not peeled), quartered. Roast for 45 minutes at 220°C/425°F/Gas 7, then transfer the bones and vegetables to a large saucepan. Pop in a bouquet garni and 6 black peppercorns. Add 2.4 litres/4 pints/10 cups water and bring to the boil. Skim, lower the heat and simmer for 4 hours, then strain. Cool, chill, then lift off the congealed fat.

CHICKEN STOCK

Break up a chicken carcass and put it in a large pan. Chop 1 onion, 1 carrot, 4 leeks and 2 celery sticks. Add to the pan with a bouquet garni, 8 black peppercorns and 2.5ml/½ tsp salt.

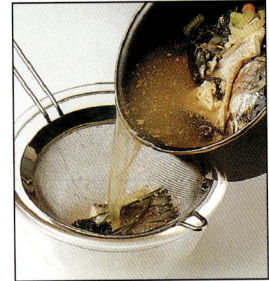

Pour in 1.75 litres/3 pints/7½ cups water. Boil, skim, then simmer for 2 hours. Degrease as for beef stock.

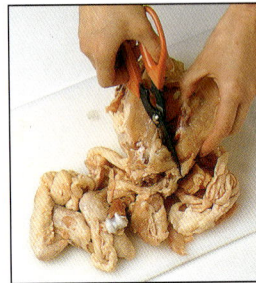

FISH STOCK

Put about 500g/1¼lb fish trimmings (bones and skin – not gills) in a saucepan. Add 1 sliced onion, 1 sliced celery stick and 6 white peppercorns. Pour in 1.5 litres/2½ pints/6¼ cups water. Boil, blot the surface, then simmer for 20 minutes and strain.

Techniques

THICKENING A SAUCE

The simplest way to thicken a liquid, at the same time intensifying the flavours, is to boil it vigorously until it reduces to the required consistency. If a liquid contains vegetables, these can be puréed for use as a thickener, but the most common way of thickening a sauce is to use flour. This can be done at the start of cooking, by melting butter slowly, then quickly stirring in flour and letting the mixture (roux) cook briefly before gradually adding the liquid. Allowing the roux to cook for longer will produce a more intense colour and flavour – the basic roux blanc is cooked for 2 minutes, the roux blond for 4 minutes and the roux brun for 8 minutes. If preferred, equal amounts of butter and flour can be mixed to a paste (beurre manié), and small amounts of the mixture can be stirred into the liquid at the end of cooking.

ALTERNATIVE THICKENERS

Cornflour can be used to thicken a liquid towards the end of cooking. Mix the required amount in a bowl with cold water to form a paste, then stir it into the hot liquid, a little at a time, and continue to stir as the sauce boils and thickens. Allow the sauce to simmer over a gentle heat for 2 minutes before serving.

Arrowroot is used in the same way as cornflour. It gives a clearer result and is favoured for sweet fruit sauces. Less stable than cornflour, it should be removed from the heat as soon as it thickens.

Egg yolks add colour and flavour while thickening a sauce. It is usual to beat the eggs with a little of the hot sauce before introducing them to the pan. Cook briefly over a low heat.

Clockwise from top left: roux blanc, roux blond, roux brun, beurre manié (centre), cornflour, egg yolks, arrowroot.

Classic Sauces

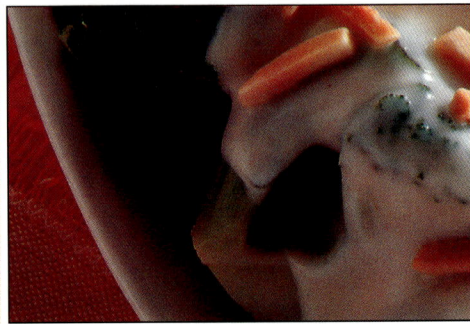

White Sauce

INGREDIENTS

600ml/1 pint/2½ cups milk
50g/2oz/4 tbsp butter
50g/2oz/½ cup plain flour
salt and ground black pepper

SERVES 6
(about 600ml/1 pint/2½ cups)

1 Warm the milk in a saucepan over a low heat. Do not let it boil. Alternatively, heat it in a jug in the microwave on High for 1 minute.

2 Melt the butter in a separate saucepan. Stir in the flour and cook over a low heat for 1–2 minutes, stirring frequently.

3 Remove the pan from the heat and add the hot milk a little at a time. Keep stirring constantly as you add the milk to prevent the mixture from becoming lumpy.

4 Return the pan to the heat and continue to stir until it boils and thickens, then lower the heat and simmer, still stirring, for 3–4 minutes. Add salt and pepper to taste, with any chosen flavouring.

VARIATIONS

To make a cheese sauce, stir in 50g/2oz/½ cup grated mature Cheddar or Red Leicester cheese, with 2.5ml/½ tsp prepared mustard. For parsley sauce, stir in 15ml/1 tbsp chopped fresh parsley.

13

Béchamel Sauce

INGREDIENTS

1 onion
1 carrot
1 celery stick
600ml / 1 pint / 2½ cups milk
1 bouquet garni
6 black peppercorns
pinch of freshly grated nutmeg or blade of mace
50g / 2oz / 4 tbsp butter
50g / 2oz / ½ cup plain flour
60ml / 4 tbsp single cream
salt and ground black pepper

SERVES 6
(about 600ml / 1 pint / 2½ cups)

1 Peel the onion, carrot and celery and chop them finely. Pour in the milk and put the vegetables into a saucepan. Add the bouquet garni, peppercorns and the nutmeg or mace. Bring to the boil, remove from the heat and leave to infuse for 30 minutes.

2 Melt the butter in a separate saucepan, stir in the flour and cook over a low heat for 1–2 minutes, stirring frequently.

3 Meanwhile, re-heat the flavoured milk. Just before it boils, remove it from the heat and strain it into a heatproof jug, pressing the vegetables with the back of a spoon to extract the maximum flavour.

4 Off the heat, gradually add the flavoured milk to the roux, stirring all the time. Return to the heat and stir until it boils and thickens, then lower the heat and simmer, still stirring, for 3–4 minutes. Just before serving, remove the bouquet garni and stir in the cream, adding salt and pepper to taste.

COOK'S TIP
To give a contrast in texture, sprinkle toasted flaked almonds or crisply fried buttered breadcrumbs over the sauce just before serving.

14

Velvety Pouring Sauce

16

INGREDIENTS

600ml / 1 pint / 2½ cups chicken or fish stock
25g / 1oz / 2 tbsp butter
25g / 1oz / ¼ cup plain flour
30ml / 2 tbsp single cream
salt and ground black pepper

SERVES 6
(about 600ml / 1 pint / 2½ cups)

1 Warm the stock in a saucepan over a low heat. Do not allow it to boil. Alternatively, heat the stock in a jug in the microwave on High for I minute.

2 Melt the butter in a separate saucepan, stir in the flour and cook over a low heat for 3–4 minutes or until it is a pale straw colour, stirring frequently to prevent it from becoming lumpy.

3 Remove the pan from the heat and gradually add the hot stock, stirring constantly. Return the pan to the heat and bring to the boil, stirring constantly, then lower

the heat and simmer until the sauce has reduced by about a quarter. Using a large spoon, skim off the fat from the surface from time to time.

4 Just before serving, remove the sauce from the heat and stir in the single cream, adding salt and pepper to taste.

Bread Sauce

INGREDIENTS

1 small onion
4 cloves
1 bay leaf
300ml/½ pint/1¼ cups milk
115g/4oz/2 cups fresh white breadcrumbs
15g/½oz/1 tbsp butter
15ml/1 tbsp single cream
salt and ground white pepper

SERVES 6
(about 475ml/16fl oz/2 cups)

1 Peel the onion and stick the cloves into it. Put the onion in a saucepan and add the bay leaf. Pour in the milk.

2 Bring the milk to the boil, then remove the pan from the heat and leave the contents to infuse for 30 minutes. Remove the onion and bay leaf from the pan.

3 Stir in the breadcrumbs, then return the pan to the heat and simmer for 4–5 minutes until the sauce is thick and creamy. Stir in the butter and cream. Add salt and pepper to taste.

COOK'S TIP

To make the sauce in the microwave, cook the clove-studded onion (without any liquid) in a glass measuring jug on High for 2 minutes, then add the bay leaf and milk. Cook for 3–4 minutes more, then remove the onion and bay leaf and stir in the crumbs. Cook for 2 minutes more, stir well and season.

Hollandaise Sauce

INGREDIENTS

115g/4oz/½ cup butter, softened
30ml/2 tbsp white wine or tarragon vinegar
15ml/1 tbsp water
6 black peppercorns
1 bay leaf
2 egg yolks
salt and ground black pepper
15–30ml/1–2 tbsp single cream (optional)

SERVES 2–3
(about 200ml/7fl oz/scant 1 cup)

3 Whisk the egg yolks into the reduced vinegar mixture. Place the bowl over the simmering water and continue to whisk until the mixture is light and fluffy. Gradually whisk in the butter, a tiny piece at a time, making sure that each piece has been absorbed completely before adding the next.

4 When the sauce has become thick and glossy, add salt and pepper to taste. If it tastes too sharp, add a little more butter. If it is too thick, whisk in the single cream. Serve immediately, with asparagus, broccoli or steamed fish.

1 Beat the butter in a bowl until it is creamy. Have ready a saucepan of simmering water, and a heatproof bowl which will fit over the top of it.

2 Combine the vinegar, water, peppercorns and bay leaf in a small saucepan. Simmer gently until the liquid has reduced by half. Strain into the heatproof bowl and leave to cool.

COOK'S TIP
For a cheat's Hollandaise, combine 3 egg yolks, 30ml/2 tbsp lemon juice and a pinch each of salt and cayenne pepper in a blender or food processor. Pulse to mix, then, with the motor running, gradually add 115g/4oz/ ½ cup melted butter through the lid or feeder tube until the mixture is thick and creamy.

Horseradish Sauce

INGREDIENTS

7.5cm / 3in piece of fresh horseradish
15ml / 1 tbsp lemon juice
10ml / 2 tsp granulated sugar
2.5ml / ½ tsp mustard powder
150ml / ¼ pint / ⅔ cup double cream

SERVES 6
(about 175ml / 6fl oz / ¾ cup)

1 Thoroughly scrub the horse-radish and remove the peel using a sharp kitchen knife or vegetable peeler. Grate the horseradish as finely as possible.

2 Mix the grated horseradish with the lemon juice, sugar and mustard powder in a bowl. In a separate bowl, whip the cream to soft peaks. Gently fold in the horseradish mixture.

COOK'S TIP
Stir a small spoonful of horseradish sauce into the dressing for a prawn cocktail, or try it with smoked mackerel or trout — although it is traditionally served with roast beef, horse-radish sauce is very good with all but the most delicate seafood.

20

Cranberry Sauce

INGREDIENTS

1 orange
225g/8oz/1½ cups cranberries, thawed
if frozen
275g/10oz/1¼ cups granulated sugar
150ml/¼ pint/⅔ cup water

SERVES 6
(about 250ml/8fl oz/1 cup)

21

1 Carefully pare the rind from the orange, in a single long strip, if possible. Using a sharp knife, scrape off any pith, then place the rind in a small saucepan. Squeeze the juice and add it to the pan, with the cranberries, sugar and water.

2 Heat gently, stirring with a wooden spoon until all the sugar has dissolved, then bring the mixture to the boil. Lower the heat and simmer for 10–15 minutes or until the berries have burst.

3 Remove the rind. Spoon the sauce into a bowl and allow to cool before serving. If a smooth sauce is preferred, rub it through a sieve before serving.

COOK'S TIP

Cranberry sauce is the traditional accompaniment for roast turkey. It looks wonderful served in pastry cases, or in hollowed-out lemon or lime cups.

Sauces for
Meat & Poultry

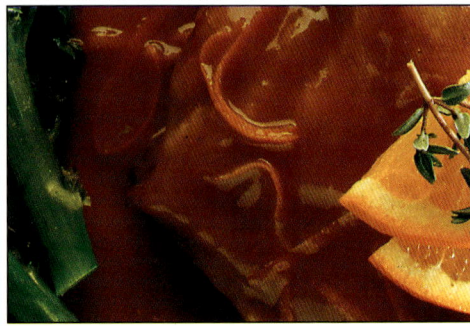

Mint Sauce

INGREDIENTS

1 small bunch of fresh mint
15ml / 1 tbsp granulated sugar
30ml / 2 tbsp boiling water
45ml / 3 tbsp white wine vinegar

SERVES 6
(about 120ml / 4fl oz / ½ cup)

1 Wash and dry the fresh mint sprigs, then strip the leaves from the stalks and pile them on a chopping board.

2 Using a sharp cook's knife, chop the leaves very finely. The easiest way to do this is to anchor the tip of the knife on the board with one hand, while moving the blade evenly up and down with the other. From time to time, gather the leaves together and change the position of the knife.

3 Scrape the chopped leaves into a bowl and add the sugar. Pour on the boiling water and leave to stand for 5–10 minutes.

4 Stir in the vinegar. If time permits, leave to stand again for 1–2 hours before serving.

COOK'S TIP
If you prefer, sprinkle the sugar over the fresh mint leaves before chopping them. Some cooks swear this improves the grip of the knife and makes the task of chopping the mint much easier.

Béarnaise Sauce

INGREDIENTS

115g/4oz/½ cup butter, softened
45ml/3 tbsp white wine vinegar
30ml/2 tbsp water
1 small onion, finely chopped
a few fresh tarragon and chervil sprigs
1 bay leaf
6 black peppercorns, crushed
2 egg yolks
15ml/1 tbsp chopped fresh herbs,
such as tarragon, parsley and chervil
salt and ground black pepper

SERVES 2–3
(about 250ml/8fl oz/1 cup)

1 Beat the butter in a bowl until it is creamy. Have ready a saucepan of simmering water, and a heat-proof bowl which will fit over the top of it.

2 Combine the vinegar, water, onion, herb sprigs, bay leaf and peppercorns in a small saucepan. Simmer gently until the liquid has reduced by half. Strain into the heatproof bowl and cool.

3 Whisk the egg yolks into the reduced vinegar mixture. Place the bowl over the simmering water and continue to whisk until the mixture is light and fluffy.

Gradually whisk in the butter, a tiny piece at a time, making sure that each piece has been absorbed completely before adding the next.

4 When the sauce is thick and glossy, add the chopped herbs, with salt and pepper to taste. Serve warm, not hot, to accompany grilled steak.

Spicy Redcurrant Sauce

INGREDIENTS

1 lemon
1 orange
2 sugar lumps
150ml/¼ pint/⅔ cup port
4 allspice berries
4 cloves
5ml/1 tsp mustard seeds
225g/8oz/scant 1 cup redcurrant jelly
10ml/2 tsp arrowroot
30ml/2 tbsp orange liqueur
pinch of ground ginger

SERVES 8
(about 475ml/16fl oz/2 cups)

1 Carefully pare the rind from the lemon. Using a sharp knife, scrape off any pith, then cut the rind into matchstick strips. Place the strips in a small saucepan, add water to cover and bring to the boil. Cook for 5 minutes, then drain the strips and set them aside.

2 Wash and dry the orange, then rub it all over with the sugar lumps until they are saturated with the orange oil. Put them in the clean pan with the port and whole spices. Bring to the boil, then remove from the heat and cool.

3 Strain the spiced port into a separate saucepan, then add the redcurrant jelly and stir over a low heat until the jelly has dissolved. Mix the arrowroot with the orange liqueur in a small jug, stir the mixture into the sauce and bring to the boil. Cook for 1–2 minutes, stirring, until the sauce is thick and smooth.

4 As soon as the sauce has thickened, remove the pan from the heat and stir in the blanched lemon rinds and the ground ginger. Serve at room temperature, with hot or cold gammon slices or grilled lamb cutlets.

Tangy Orange Sauce

INGREDIENTS

*2 Seville oranges or 2 sweet oranges plus
10ml/2 tsp lemon juice
25g/1oz/2 tbsp butter or roasting pan juices
40g/1½oz/6 tbsp plain flour
300ml/½ pint/1¼ cups hot stock
(preferably duck)
150ml/¼ pint/⅔ cup red wine
15ml/1 tbsp orange liqueur
30ml/2 tbsp redcurrant jelly
salt and ground black pepper*

SERVES 6
(about 600ml/1 pint/2½ cups)

1 Pare the rind from one of the oranges. Using a sharp knife, scrape off any pith, then cut the rind into matchstick strips. Place it in a saucepan, add water to cover and bring to the boil. Cook for 5 minutes, then drain the strips and set them aside. Squeeze both oranges into a bowl and add the lemon juice if using.

2 Melt the butter in a small saucepan. Alternatively, pour off any excess fat from the roasting pan, leaving the juices. Then sprinkle in the flour and cook, stirring constantly, for about 4 minutes or until lightly browned.

3 Over a low heat, gradually stir in the hot stock and wine. Bring to the boil, stirring all the time, then lower the heat and simmer for 5 minutes.

4 Add the orange juice, orange rinds, liqueur and redcurrant jelly to the sauce. Stir over a low heat until the jelly has dissolved, then add salt and pepper to taste. Serve at once, poured over jointed roast duckling or game.

COOK'S TIP

For a simple but impressive supper for friends, grill venison sausages and serve them with this delectable sauce. Add some pan-fried potatoes and braised red cabbage.

Mushroom & Wine Sauce

INGREDIENTS

115g/4oz/1 cup button mushrooms
50g/2oz/4 tbsp butter
3 rindless streaky bacon rashers, chopped
1 carrot, chopped
1 celery stick, chopped
3 shallots, finely chopped
25g/1oz/¼ cup plain flour
600ml/1 pint/2½ cups hot brown stock
1 bouquet garni
30ml/2 tbsp tomato purée
120ml/4fl oz/½ cup white wine
30ml/2 tbsp brandy
15ml/1 tbsp chopped fresh parsley
salt and ground black pepper

SERVES 4–6
(about 750ml/1¼ pints/3 cups)

1 Remove the mushroom stalks and chop them finely; slice the caps and set them aside. Melt half the butter in a heavy-based saucepan and fry the bacon for 2–3 minutes. Add the finely chopped mushroom stalks, with the carrot and celery, then stir in two-thirds of the chopped shallots. Fry for 5 minutes until the vegetables are lightly browned.

2 Stir in the flour and cook over a medium heat for 5–10 minutes, until it is a rich brown colour. Add the stock gradually, stirring until the sauce boils and thickens. Add the bouquet garni and tomato purée. Simmer for 1 hour, stirring occasionally.

3 Heat the remaining butter in a small pan and fry the remaining shallots until softened. Add the reserved mushroom slices and sauté until beginning to brown, then pour in the wine and brandy. Simmer until the liquid is reduced by half. Stir the wine mixture into the sauce. Add the parsley, then season with salt and pepper. Heat through, stirring occasionally. Remove the bouquet garni and serve with grilled or roast pork or chicken.

Sweet & Sour Sauce

INGREDIENTS

1 carrot
1 green pepper
15ml / 1 tbsp vegetable oil
1 small onion, chopped
1 garlic clove, crushed
2.5cm / 1in piece of fresh root ginger, grated
15ml / 1 tbsp cornflour
300ml / ½ pint / 1¼ cups chicken stock
30ml / 2 tbsp tomato purée
15ml / 1 tbsp soft dark brown sugar
30ml / 2 tbsp white wine vinegar
30ml / 2 tbsp rice wine or dry sherry
salt and ground black pepper

SERVES 4
(about 350ml / 12fl oz / 1½ cups)

1 Slice the carrot lengthways, then cut it into thin strips. Quarter the pepper, discard the core and seeds and cut the flesh into thin strips.

2 Heat the oil in a saucepan and fry the onion and garlic for 5 minutes until soft but not brown. Add the carrot and pepper strips, with the ginger. Fry for 1 minute more.

3 In a small bowl, mix the cornflour to a paste with a little of the chicken stock. Pour the remaining stock into the pan, then stir in the tomato purée, brown sugar, vinegar and rice wine or sherry.

4 Add the cornflour paste to the pan. Stir over a medium heat until the sauce boils and thickens. Lower the heat and simmer for 2–3 minutes or until the vegetables are just tender. Add salt and pepper to taste. Serve with stir-fried pork, prawns or chicken, garnished with cucumber, or pour the sauce over rice or noodles.

29

Green Peppercorn Sauce

Ingredients

15ml / 1 tbsp green peppercorns in brine, drained
40g / 1½ oz / 3 tbsp butter
1 small onion, finely chopped
300ml / ½ pint / 1¼ cups chicken
or vegetable stock
juice of ½ lemon
15ml / 1 tbsp plain flour
5ml / 1 tsp Dijon mustard
45ml / 3 tbsp double cream
salt and ground black pepper

Serves 3–4
(about 350ml / 12fl oz / 1½ cups)

1 Pat the peppercorns dry on kitchen paper, then use the flat blade of a sharp knife to crush them.

2 Melt 25g/1oz/2 tbsp of the butter in a small saucepan. Add the onion and cook over a low heat for 3–4 minutes, then add the stock and lemon juice. Bring to the boil, lower the heat and simmer for 15 minutes.

3 Then soften the remaining butter, if necessary, and work in the flour to make a paste (beurre manié). Pinch off tiny pieces of the paste and stir them into the sauce, making sure that each piece has been absorbed before adding the next. Cook until the sauce thickens.

4 Lower the heat and whisk in the peppercorns, mustard and cream, with salt and pepper to taste. Serve hot, with pork steaks, buttered pasta or rabbit.

Barbecue Sauce

INGREDIENTS

30ml/2 tbsp vegetable oil
1 large onion, chopped
2 garlic cloves, crushed
400g/14oz can tomatoes
30ml/2 tbsp Worcestershire sauce
15ml/1 tbsp white wine vinegar
45ml/3 tbsp clear honey
5ml/1 tsp mustard powder
2.5ml/½ tsp mild chilli powder (optional)
salt and ground black pepper

SERVES 4
(about 350ml/12fl oz/1½ cups)

1 Heat the oil in a saucepan and fry the onion with the garlic until soft. Stir in the canned tomatoes, Worcestershire sauce, white wine vinegar, honey and mustard powder. Add the chilli powder, if you are using it, and mix well.

2 Simmer the sauce, uncovered, for 15–20 minutes, stirring occasionally, until it is thick and flavoursome. Cool slightly, then purée in a blender or food processor. If a very smooth sauce is preferred, press the mixture through a sieve into a clean bowl. Add salt and pepper to taste.

3 Pour the sauce into a bowl and serve hot or cold, with hot dogs or burgers. Barbecue sauce is also very good for basting: brush it over chops, steaks, chicken drumsticks or kebabs before cooking them on the barbecue.

31

Lemon & Tarragon Sauce

INGREDIENTS

1 lemon
small bunch of fresh tarragon
1 shallot, finely chopped
90ml/6 tbsp white wine
1 quantity Velvety Pouring Sauce, page 16
45ml/3 tbsp double cream
30ml/2 tbsp brandy
salt and ground black pepper

SERVES 6
(about 750ml/1¼ pints/3 cups)

1 Carefully pare the rind from the lemon. Using a sharp knife, scrape off any pith, then place the rind in a small saucepan. Squeeze the juice and add it to the pan.

2 Strip the tarragon leaves from the stalks and chop them finely using a sharp knife. Set aside 15ml/1tbsp, then add the remaining chopped leaves to the saucepan, with the chopped shallot and white wine. Bring the mixture to simmering point and cook until it has reduced by half.

3 Strain the tarragon and wine mixture through a fine sieve into a larger saucepan and add the pouring sauce. Mix well, then stir in the cream, brandy and reserved tarragon. Heat through without boiling, add salt and pepper to taste, then pour into a serving jug or gravy boat. Serve with chicken, or, alternatively, with egg or steamed vegetable dishes.

Satay Sauce

INGREDIENTS

150g/5oz/1¼ cups roasted unsalted peanuts
45ml/3 tbsp vegetable oil
1 small onion, roughly chopped
2 garlic cloves, chopped
1 fresh red chilli, seeded and chopped
2.5cm/1in piece of fresh root ginger,
peeled and chopped
5cm/2in piece of lemon grass, roughly chopped
2.5ml/½ tsp ground cumin
45ml/3 tbsp chopped fresh coriander
15ml/1 tbsp sesame oil
175ml/6fl oz/¾ cup coconut milk
30ml/2 tbsp kecap manis (thick soy sauce)
10ml/2 tsp freshly squeezed lime juice
salt and ground black pepper

SERVES 6
(about 350ml/12fl oz/1½ cups)

1 Place the peanuts in a clean dish towel and rub off the husks. Tip into a food processor and add 30ml/2 tbsp of the vegetable oil. Grind to a smooth paste. Scrape into a bowl and set aside.

2 Add the onion, garlic, chilli, ginger, lemon grass, cumin and coriander to the clean food processor. Process to a fairly smooth paste.

33

3 Heat the remaining vegetable oil with the sesame oil in a small saucepan. Add the onion paste and cook over a low heat for 10–15 minutes, stirring occasionally. Stir in the peanut paste, with the coconut milk, kecap manis (thick soy sauce) and lime juice. Heat through gently, stirring all the time with a wooden spoon.

4 Add salt and pepper to taste. Spoon the sauce into six individual bowls or saucers and serve warm with grilled skewered chicken or pork, garnished with lettuce leaves, lime wedges and fresh chives. Satay sauce also makes an excellent dip for small spicy meatballs.

Sauces for Fish

Creamy Dill & Mustard Sauce

INGREDIENTS

25g / 1oz / 2 tbsp butter
20g / ¾oz / 3 tbsp plain flour
300ml / ½ pint / 1¼ cups hot fish stock
15ml / 1 tbsp white wine vinegar
45ml / 3 tbsp chopped fresh dill
15ml / 1 tbsp wholegrain mustard
10ml / 2 tsp granulated sugar
2 egg yolks
salt and ground black pepper

SERVES 4
(about 400ml / 14fl oz / 1⅔ cups)

1 Melt the butter in a saucepan. Stir in the flour and cook for 1–2 minutes over a low heat, stirring constantly. Off the heat, gradually stir in the hot stock.

2 Return the pan to the heat. Bring to the boil, stirring all the time, then lower the heat and simmer for 2–3 minutes. Remove from the heat again and beat in the vinegar, dill, mustard and sugar.

3 Using a fork, beat the egg yolks in a small bowl. Gradually add a small quantity of the hot sauce. Add the contents of the bowl to the sauce, whisking vigorously. Place the pan back on the stove and continue to whisk the sauce over a very low heat for 1 minute more. Add salt and pepper to taste. Serve at once, with grilled sole, plaice or brill.

35

COOK'S TIP
When buying the fish to serve with this sauce, ask the supplier for the trimmings. Use them to make the fish stock.

Watercress Cream

INGREDIENTS

2 bunches watercress
150ml / ¼ pint / ⅔ cup hot fish stock
150ml / ¼ pint / ⅔ cup dry white wine
25g / 1oz / 2 tbsp butter
2 shallots, chopped
25g / 1oz / ¼ cup plain flour
5ml / 1 tsp anchovy essence
150ml / ¼ pint / ⅔ cup single cream
salt and cayenne pepper
lemon juice

SERVES 4–6
(about 600ml / 1 pint / 2½ cups)

1 Remove bruised leaves and coarse stalks from the watercress. Bring a saucepan of lightly salted water to the boil and blanch the watercress for 5 minutes.

2 Drain the watercress, refresh under cold running water, then drain again. Press against the sides of the sieve or colander to extract as much liquid as possible, then tip on to a board and chop finely.

3 Mix the stock and wine in a jug. Melt the butter in a saucepan. Fry the shallots for about 4 minutes until soft, then stir in the flour and cook for 1 minute. Turn the heat to the lowest setting and gradually stir in the stock and wine. Raise the heat and bring the sauce to the boil, stirring constantly, then simmer for 2–3 minutes.

4 Strain the sauce into a clean saucepan. Stir in the watercress, anchovy essence and cream, with salt and cayenne to taste. Warm through over a very low heat. Just before serving, sharpen the flavour of the sauce with a little lemon juice. Serve immediately, with grilled or poached salmon or salmon trout.

COOK'S TIP
Watercress leaves have a naturally peppery taste, so cayenne pepper is used instead of ground black pepper for seasoning.

36

Saffron Cream

INGREDIENTS

pinch of saffron strands
30ml/2 tbsp hot water
25g/1oz/2 tbsp butter
2 shallots, finely chopped
90ml/6 tbsp dry white wine
60ml/4 tbsp double cream
2 egg yolks
1 quantity hot Velvety Pouring Sauce
(page 16), made with fish stock
salt and ground black pepper

SERVES 4–6
(about 750ml/1¼ pints/3 cups)

1 Put the saffron strands in a small bowl and add the hot water. Leave to soak for 15 minutes.

2 Melt the butter in a saucepan. Add the shallots and sauté for 5 minutes, until they soften. Add the wine and simmer gently until it is reduced by half. Strain the saffron water into the pan. Add the cream and cook over a very low heat for 2 minutes.

3 Using a fork, beat the egg yolks in a small bowl. Gradually add a small quantity of the hot pouring sauce. Add the contents of the bowl to the rest of the pouring sauce in a pan, whisking vigorously.

4 Place the pan over a low heat and continue to whisk for 2 minutes, until the pouring sauce thickens slightly. Whisk in the saffron mixture, season to taste and serve at once. This sauce is a perfect dressing for steamed scallops, served in a crisp vol-au-vent and garnished with fresh chervil.

Garlic & Chilli Dip

INGREDIENTS

1 small fresh red chilli
2.5cm / 1 in piece of fresh root ginger
2 garlic cloves, roughly chopped
5ml / 1 tsp mustard powder
15ml / 1 tbsp sweet chilli sauce
30ml / 2 tbsp olive oil
30ml / 2 tbsp light soy sauce
juice of 2 limes
30ml / 2 tbsp chopped fresh parsley
salt and ground black pepper

SERVES 4
(about 150ml / ¼ pint / ⅔ cup)

1 Cut the chilli in half, remove the seeds and chop the flesh finely. Put it in a mortar and grate in the ginger. Add the garlic and mustard powder. Using a pestle, grind the mixture to a rough paste.

2 Mix the chilli sauce, olive oil, soy sauce and lime juice in a bowl. Stir in the chilli paste. Mix well, cover with clear film and chill for 24 hours.

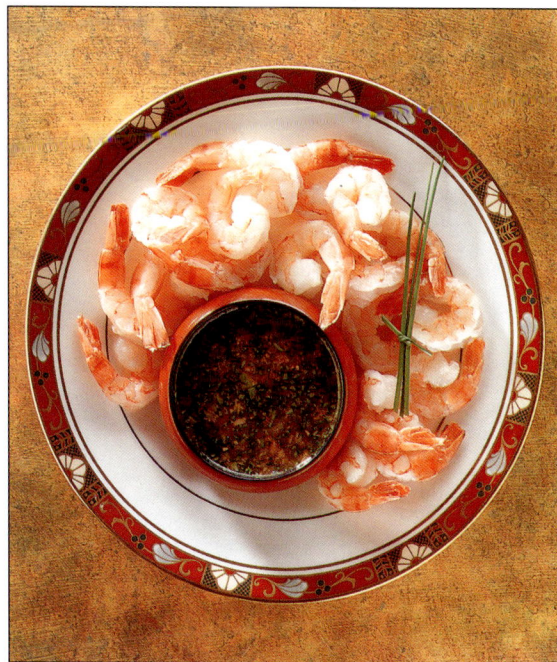

3 Stir in the parsley, with salt and pepper to taste. Serve the sauce with grilled fish, or spoon it into small bowls and serve on individual plates, with prawns for dipping. Garnish with snipped chives, if you like.

VARIATION

The dip also makes a good, flavoursome basting sauce for grilling or barbecuing. Try it on chicken or pork steaks.

39

Tartare Sauce

INGREDIENTS

2 hard-boiled eggs
1 large egg yolk
10ml/2 tsp lemon juice
175ml/6fl oz/¾ cup olive oil
5ml/1 tsp chopped drained capers
5ml/1 tsp chopped drained gherkin
5ml/1 tsp snipped fresh chives
5ml/1 tsp chopped fresh parsley
salt and ground black pepper

SERVES 6
(about 200ml/7fl oz/scant 1 cup)

1 Cut the hard-boiled eggs in half and scoop the yolks into a sieve. Use the back of a teaspoon to press them through the sieve into a bowl.

2 Stir in the raw egg yolk until smooth, then mix in the lemon juice. Add the oil very slowly, a teaspoon at a time, whisking constantly. When the sauce starts to thicken, pour in the remaining oil in a thin, steady stream, continuing to whisk until the sauce is thick and creamy.

3 Chop one egg white finely (discard the rest or save it for another dish). Stir the egg white into the sauce with the capers, gherkin and fresh herbs. Season to taste and serve with fried or grilled fish.

COOK'S TIP

This is an authentic tartare sauce. For a quick version that tastes very good, cut out Steps 1 and 2 and simply stir the flavourings into a good-quality mayonnaise.

Orange & Caper Sauce

INGREDIENTS

25g / 1oz / 2 tbsp butter
1 onion, finely chopped
fish bones and trimmings
5ml / 1 tsp black peppercorns
300ml / ½ pint / 1¼ cups dry white wine
2 small oranges
15ml / 1 tbsp drained capers
60ml / 4 tbsp crème fraîche
salt and ground black pepper

SERVES 4
(about 450ml / ¾ pint / scant 2 cups)

1 Melt the butter in a saucepan. Add the onion to the pan and sauté over a medium heat for 5 minutes or until lightly browned. Add the fish trimmings and peppercorns. Pour in the white wine and heat the mixture until it barely simmers. Cook over a gentle heat for 20 minutes.

2 Using a serrated knife, peel the oranges, taking care to remove all the pith. Working over a bowl to catch any juice, cut between the orange membranes to release the segments. Add the orange segments to the juice in the bowl.

3 Strain the fish stock into a clean pan. Add the capers and orange segments, with any juice. Bring to simmering point, then lower the heat and gently stir in the crème fraîche. Season with salt and pepper and serve at once, with grilled or poached skate wings, or plaice.

41

Sauces for
Pasta & Vegetables

Pesto

INGREDIENTS

*50g/2oz/2 cups tightly packed basil leaves
2 garlic cloves, crushed
30ml/2 tbsp pine nuts
120ml/4fl oz/½ cup olive oil
40g/1½oz/½ cup finely grated
Parmesan cheese
salt and ground black pepper*

SERVES 4
(about 300ml/½ pint/1¼ cups)

1 Combine the basil leaves, garlic cloves and pine nuts in a mortar. Using a pestle, grind them to a fine paste. Scrape the mixture into a mixing bowl and whisk in the olive oil, one teaspoon at a time.

2 Alternatively, grind the basil, garlic and nuts in a food processor. With the motor running, gradually add the oil through the feeder tube in a thin stream until the sauce is thick and smooth. Scrape into a mixing bowl.

3 Stir the cheese into the basil mixture, with salt and pepper to taste. Heat gently and toss with pasta, or serve on boiled new potatoes.

VARIATION
For tomato pesto, drain 4 sun-dried tomatoes in oil. Grind them with the basil, garlic and nuts. Substitute 60ml/4 tbsp of the oil from the tomatoes for half the olive oil.

Rich Tomato Sauce

INGREDIENTS

30ml/2 tbsp olive oil
1 large onion, chopped
2 garlic cloves, crushed
1 carrot, finely diced
1 celery stick, finely diced
675g/1½lb tomatoes, peeled and chopped
150ml/¼ pint/⅔ cup red wine
150ml/¼ pint/⅔ cup vegetable stock
1 bouquet garni
2.5ml/½ tsp granulated sugar
15ml/1 tbsp tomato purée
salt and ground black pepper

SERVES 4–6
(about 750ml/1¼ pints/3 cups)

44

1 Heat the oil in a saucepan. Add the chopped onion and crushed garlic and cook over a low heat for 10 minutes, until softened but not coloured. Add the carrot and celery and cook for 10 minutes more.

2 Stir in the tomatoes, wine and stock. Add the bouquet garni to the pan, with salt and pepper to taste. Bring to the boil, lower the heat, cover and simmer for 45 minutes, stirring occasionally.

3 Remove the bouquet garni and adjust the seasoning, adding sugar and tomato purée to taste. Serve the sauce as it is, or purée it in a blender or food processor. For a very fine sauce, press it through a sieve. Spoon over steamed courgettes or beans, serve with pasta, or use in a vegetable lasagne.

Gorgonzola & Walnut Sauce

INGREDIENTS

50g/2oz/4 tbsp butter
50g/2oz/½ cup button mushrooms, sliced
150g/5oz Gorgonzola cheese
150ml/¼ pint/⅔ cup soured cream
25g/1oz/⅓ cup grated Pecorino
or Parmesan cheese
50g/2oz/½ cup broken walnut pieces
ground black pepper

SERVES 2–3
(about 475ml/16fl oz/2 cups)

1 Melt the butter in a saucepan. Add the mushrooms and fry over a moderately high heat until lightly browned.

2 Meanwhile, put the Gorgonzola in a bowl and mash it with a fork. Stir in the soured cream and add pepper to taste (it will probably not be necessary to add salt).

3 Stir the Gorgonzola mixture into the mushrooms and heat gently until the cheese melts and the sauce is rich and creamy. Stir in the Pecorino or Parmesan, with the walnut pieces. Tossed with pasta, this makes a marvellous meal for two or three people.

VARIATION

Slice 4 large potatoes into thin rounds. Bring a saucepan of lightly salted water to the boil, add the potato slices and cook for 3 minutes. Drain. Layer the potatoes with the sauce in a greased gratin dish. Sprinkle with more grated Pecorino or Parmesan and bake at 180°C/350°F/Gas 4 for 1 hour.

Mousseline Sauce

INGREDIENTS

2 egg yolks
15ml/1 tbsp lemon juice
75g/3oz/6 tbsp butter, softened
90ml/6 tbsp double cream
salt and ground black pepper

SERVES 4
(about 200ml/7fl oz/scant 1 cup)

46

1 Combine the egg yolks and lemon juice in a heatproof bowl. Place over barely simmering water and whisk constantly until thick and fluffy.

2 Whisk in the butter, a very small amount at a time, making sure that each piece has been absorbed before adding the next. Whisk over the heat until the sauce has the consistency of mayonnaise. Remove the bowl from the pan.

3 In a separate bowl, whip the cream until stiff. Fold it into the sauce. Add salt and pepper to taste, with a little more lemon juice if you feel the sauce needs it. Serve as a dip, with prepared artichokes or artichoke hearts.

COOK'S TIP
For a rich mousseline sauce, make up a quantity of Hollandaise Sauce, following the recipe on page 18. Fold in 90ml/6 tbsp whipped cream.

Creamy Gruyère Sauce

INGREDIENTS

40g / 1½oz / 3 tbsp butter
40g / 1½oz / 6 tbsp plain flour
450ml / ¾ pint / scant 2 cups hot vegetable
or chicken stock
2 egg yolks
5ml / 1 tsp Dijon mustard
pinch of grated nutmeg or ground mace
30ml / 2 tbsp dry sherry
75g / 3oz / ¾ cup grated Gruyère cheese

SERVES 6
(about 600ml / 1 pint / 2½ cups)

1 Melt the butter in a saucepan. Stir in the flour and cook over a medium heat for 1 minute, stirring frequently. Remove from the heat and gradually stir in the hot stock. Return to the stove and bring to the boil, stirring constantly until the sauce thickens. Lower the heat and simmer for 3–4 minutes.

2 Using a fork, beat the egg yolks in a small bowl. Gradually add a small quantity of the hot sauce. Add the contents of the bowl to the sauce, stirring vigorously. Continue to whisk over a very low heat for about 2 minutes.

3 Stir in the mustard and nutmeg or mace, with the sherry and grated cheese. Add salt and pepper to taste. As soon as the cheese has melted, serve over steamed broccoli, cauliflower or leeks. The sauce also goes well with pasta, with 4 crumbled grilled bacon rashers added, if you like.

Marinades & Salsas

Red Wine & Juniper Marinade

INGREDIENTS

2 carrots, cut into batons
225g/8oz baby onions or shallots
115g/4oz/1 cup button mushrooms
4 rosemary sprigs
8 juniper berries, lightly crushed
8 black peppercorns, lightly crushed
300ml/½ pint/1¼ cups red wine
30ml/2 tbsp vegetable oil
150ml/¼ pint/⅔ cup beef stock
15g/½oz/1 tbsp butter
15ml/1 tbsp plain flour
FOR MARINATING AND COOKING
675g/1½lb boned leg of lamb, trimmed and
cut into 2.5cm/1 in cubes

SERVES 6
(475ml/16fl oz/2 cups marinade)

1 Put the meat for marinating in a large bowl. Add the vegetables, rosemary, juniper berries and peppercorns. Pour over the wine. Mix well, cover and chill for 4–5 hours, stirring occasionally.

2 Using a slotted spoon, transfer the meat and vegetables to a plate. Strain the marinade into a jug.

3 Preheat the oven to 160°C/325°F/Gas 3. Heat the oil in a large frying pan. Fry the meat and vegetables in batches. As each batch browns, transfer it to a flameproof casserole. Pour over the marinade and the stock. Cover and bake for 1½ hours.

4 Soften the butter, if necessary, then work in the flour to make a paste (beurre manié). Transfer the casserole to the top of the stove, placing it over a medium heat. Pinch off tiny pieces of the paste and stir them into the casserole, a little at a time, making sure that each piece has been absorbed before adding the next. Cook until the sauce thickens. Season to taste. Return the casserole to the oven for 30 minutes more before serving.

49

Summer Herb Marinade

INGREDIENTS

*fresh herb sprigs (chervil, thyme, parsley,
sage, chives, rosemary, oregano)*
90ml/6 tbsp olive oil
45ml/3 tbsp tarragon vinegar
1 garlic clove, crushed
2 spring onions, chopped
salt and ground black pepper
FOR MARINATING AND COOKING
*4 pork steaks, chicken portions, salmon cutlets
or lamb chops*

SERVES 4
(about 150ml/¼ pint/⅔ cup marinade)

50

1 Remove any coarse stalks or damaged leaves from the herbs. Chop the remaining leaves finely, tip into a bowl and add the oil, vinegar, garlic and spring onions, with salt and pepper to taste. Mix well.

2 Place the meat or fish in another bowl and pour over the marinade. Cover the bowl with clear film and chill for 4–6 hours, stirring occasionally.

3 Preheat the grill or light the barbecue. When ready, lift the meat or fish out of the marinade and grill or barbecue until cooked through, basting occasionally with the remaining marinade.

COOK'S TIP
*If you are cooking the meat or fish on
the barbecue, take care when basting,
as any marinade that drips on to the
hot coals will instantly cause the
fire to flare.*

Ginger & Lime Marinade

INGREDIENTS

3 limes
15ml / 1 tbsp green cardamom pods
1 onion, finely chopped
2.5cm / 1 in piece of fresh root ginger, grated
1 large garlic clove, crushed
45ml / 3 tbsp olive oil

KEBABS

225g / 8oz raw prawns, peeled and deveined
225g / 8oz monkfish tail, cubed
selection of prepared vegetables and herbs
(peppers, courgettes, button mushrooms,
red onion wedges, cherry tomatoes and bay leaves)

SERVES 4–6
(about 90ml / 6 tbsp marinade)

1 Finely grate the rind from 1 of the limes, then squeeze the juice from all 3 limes. Split the cardamom pods and scrape out the seeds into a mortar. Discard the pods and, using a pestle, crush the seeds finely.

2 Tip the ground cardamom seeds into a jug. Add the lime rind and juice, with the onion, grated ginger and garlic. Gradually whisk in the oil. Put the fish and shellfish for the kebabs in a bowl, pour over the marinade and mix gently. Cover and marinate for 2–3 hours in a cool place.

3 Preheat the grill or light the barbecue. When ready, remove the fish and shellfish from the marinade, using a slotted spoon. Thread them, with the chosen vegetables and herbs, on four skewers. Grill under a medium heat or over medium-hot coals, basting occasionally with the marinade.

Spicy Yogurt Marinade

INGREDIENTS

5ml / 1 tsp coriander seeds
10ml / 2 tsp cumin seeds
6 cloves
2 bay leaves
1 onion, quartered
2 garlic cloves, roughly chopped
5cm / 2in piece of fresh root ginger, peeled
and roughly chopped
2.5ml / ½ tsp chilli powder
5ml / 1 tsp ground turmeric
150ml / ¼ pint / ⅔ cup natural yogurt
FOR MARINATING AND COOKING
6 chicken pieces, skinned
juice of 1 lemon
5ml / 1 tsp salt
lemon or lime wedges, salad leaves and
fresh herbs, to serve

SERVES 6
(about 175ml / 6fl oz / ¾ cup marinade)

1 Prepare the chicken for marinating by making several deep slashes in the fleshiest parts with a sharp knife. Arrange the chicken pieces in a single layer in a shallow dish, sprinkle over the lemon juice and salt and rub in. Cover with clear film while you make the marinade.

2 Spread out the coriander and cumin seeds in a frying pan. Add the cloves and bay leaves. Dry roast over a medium heat until the seeds are fragrant and the bay leaves have become crisp. Tip the roasted spices into a mortar. Leave to cool, then grind to a coarse powder, using a pestle.

3 Pulse the onion, garlic and ginger in a food processor until finely chopped. Add the ground spice mix, with the chilli powder, turmeric and yogurt, then add the lemon juice from the chicken. Process briefly to mix.

4 Arrange the chicken pieces in a single layer in a roasting tin. Pour over the marinade, making sure that each piece of chicken is coated. Cover the roasting tin with clear film and chill for 24 hours, turning occasionally.

5 Preheat the oven to 200°C/400°F/Gas 6. Bake the marinated chicken for about 45 minutes. Serve hot or cold, with lemon or lime wedges, salad leaves and fresh herbs.

Tomato Salsa

INGREDIENTS

6 tomatoes
1 fresh green chilli
2 spring onions, chopped
10cm/4in piece of cucumber, diced
30ml/2 tbsp lemon juice
30ml/2 tbsp chopped fresh coriander
15ml/1 tbsp chopped fresh parsley
salt and ground black pepper

SERVES 6
(about 300ml/½ pint/1¼ cups)

1 Cut a cross in the stalk end of each tomato. Place in a bowl and pour over boiling water to cover. Leave for 1 minute, until the skins start to split. Drain and plunge into cold water. Slip off the skins. Quarter the tomatoes, squeeze out the seeds and dice the flesh.

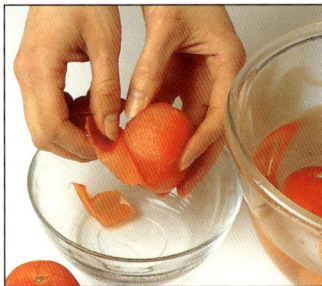

2 Cut the chilli in half lengthways, scrape out the seeds and dice the flesh. Place in a bowl, with the tomatoes, spring onions, cucumber, lemon juice and herbs. Mix well and add salt and pepper. Cover and chill for 1–2 hours before serving.

VARIATIONS

Tomato & Caper Salsa: Mix 6 diced tomatoes, 15ml/1 tbsp chopped drained capers, 2 chopped spring onions, the shredded leaves from 6 basil sprigs, 30ml/2 tbsp lime juice and salt and pepper.

Tomato & Roast Pepper Salsa: Roast 1 orange pepper and dice. Mix with 6 diced tomatoes, 30ml/2 tbsp lemon juice, a crushed garlic clove, salt and pepper.

Guacamole

INGREDIENTS

2 large ripe avocados
1 small onion, finely chopped
1 garlic clove, crushed
juice of ½ lemon
15ml / 1 tbsp olive oil
2 tomatoes
pinch of ground coriander
few drops of Tabasco sauce
salt and ground black pepper
cayenne pepper, for sprinkling

SERVES 6
(about 300ml / ½ pint / 1¼ cups)

1 Cut the avocados in half, remove the stones and scoop the flesh into a large bowl. Mash until smooth, then beat in the onion and garlic.

2 Add the lemon juice and oil to the avocado purée, mixing well. Peel the tomatoes as described in Step 1 of Tomato Salsa (page 54), squeeze out the seeds and chop the flesh finely. Stir the tomatoes into the avocado mixture.

3 Season the guacamole with the coriander, Tabasco, salt and black pepper. Spoon into small bowls and sprinkle with the cayenne. Serve with corn chips and crisp vegetables for dipping, or serve as a sauce with chilli and hot tortillas.

COOK'S TIP
Avocado flesh discolours quickly. The lemon juice will help to keep it green, but it should be served as soon as possible. If you must keep it, cover the surface closely with clear film.

Roasted Pepper & Ginger Salsa

INGREDIENTS

1 large red pepper
1 large yellow pepper
1 large orange pepper
2.5cm / 1in piece of fresh root ginger
2.5ml / ½ tsp coriander seeds
5ml / 1 tsp cumin seeds
1 small garlic clove, chopped
30ml / 2 tbsp lemon or fresh lime juice
1 small red onion, finely chopped
30ml / 2 tbsp chopped fresh coriander
5ml / 1 tsp chopped fresh thyme
salt and ground black pepper

SERVES 6
(about 350ml / 12fl oz / 1½ cups)

1 Preheat the grill. Using a sharp knife, cut each pepper into quarters. Remove the stalks, seeds and membranes and arrange the quarters, skin side up, in the grill pan. Grill the peppers until the skins are charred and blistered.

2 Rub off the pepper skins and slice the flesh very finely. If the skins are difficult to remove, put the grilled halves in a bowl and cover with several layers of kitchen paper. Leave for 10 minutes, then rub off the skins.

3 Peel the root ginger, chop it roughly and set it aside. Dry roast the coriander and cumin seeds in a frying pan for 30 seconds, until fragrant.

4 Tip the roasted spices into a mortar and add the ginger and garlic. Using a pestle, grind the mixture to a pulp. Work in the fresh lemon or lime juice.

5 Scrape the contents of the mortar into a bowl and add the peppers, onion, fresh coriander and thyme. Stir in salt and pepper to taste. Mix well, cover and chill for 1–2 hours. Serve with barbecued meats or halloumi cheese kebabs.

Dessert Sauces

Classic Custard Sauce

INGREDIENTS

450ml / ¾ pint / scant 2 cups creamy milk
1 vanilla pod, split
4 egg yolks
45ml / 3 tbsp caster sugar

SERVES 6
(about 600ml / 1 pint / 2½ cups)

1 Put the milk in a saucepan with the vanilla pod. Bring slowly to just below boiling point, then remove from the heat and set aside to infuse for 10 minutes. Remove the vanilla pod.

2 Whisk the egg yolks with the caster sugar in a heatproof bowl until pale, thick and creamy. Then gradually stir in the vanilla milk with a spoon.

3 Place the bowl over a saucepan of simmering water. Stir constantly over a low heat for about 10 minutes or until the custard coats the back of the spoon. Remove from the heat immediately.

4 Strain the custard into a jug or bowl. If serving cold, cover the surface closely with clear film or buttered greaseproof paper to prevent the formation of a skin.

VARIATIONS
Infuse a few strips of thinly pared lemon or orange rind in the milk, instead of the vanilla pod, or flavour the custard with orange liqueur.

59

Chocolate Fudge Sauce

INGREDIENTS

150ml/¼ pint/⅔ cup double cream
50g/2oz/4 tbsp butter, diced
50g/2oz/¼ cup caster sugar or vanilla sugar
175g/6oz plain chocolate
30ml/2 tbsp brandy

SERVES 6
(about 350ml/12fl oz/1½ cups)

1 Combine the cream, butter and sugar in a heat-proof bowl. Place over simmering water and heat gently, stirring occasionally, until both butter and sugar have melted and the mixture is smooth. Turn off the heat and let the mixture cool slightly.

2 Break the plain chocolate into squares and add them to the cream mixture. Leave for about 5 minutes until the chocolate is soft, then stir until smooth.

3 Slowly add the brandy, stirring constantly. Pour the sauce into a jug. Serve hot over ice cream, or at room temperature over profiteroles or pancakes.

VARIATIONS
White Chocolate & Orange Sauce: Add the grated rind of 1 orange to the cream mixture. Use white chocolate instead of plain, and orange liqueur as a substitute for brandy.
Mocha Fudge Sauce: Use soft light brown sugar instead of caster sugar, and coffee liqueur instead of brandy. Stir in 15ml/1 tbsp coffee essence just before serving.

Ginger & Honey Sauce

INGREDIENTS

1 lemon
4 green cardamom pods
1 cinnamon stick
150ml / ¼ pint / ⅔ cup clear honey
*30ml / 2 tbsp ginger syrup (from the stem
ginger jar)*
60ml / 4 tbsp water
3 pieces of stem ginger

SERVES 4
(about 250ml / 8fl oz / 1 cup)

1 Carefully pare two strips of rind from the lemon. Using a sharp knife, scrape off any pith. Lightly crush the cardamom pods, using a sharp knife, held flat.

2 Combine the lemon rind and crushed cardamom pods in a saucepan. Add the cinnamon stick, honey and ginger syrup. Pour in the water. Bring to the boil, then lower the heat and simmer the syrup for 2 minutes.

3 Meanwhile, chop the stem ginger. Cut the lemon in half and squeeze the juice from one half. Stir the ginger and lemon juice into the syrup. Pour the hot sauce over a steamed pudding, or use it to dress a winter salad of poached dried fruits and sliced oranges. Chill the fruit salad before serving.

Redcurrant & Raspberry Sauce

INGREDIENTS

225g / 8oz / 1½ cups redcurrants
450g / 1lb / 3 cups raspberries, hulled
50g / 2oz / scant ½ cup icing sugar
15ml / 1 tbsp cornflour
juice of 1 orange
30ml / 2 tbsp double cream

SERVES 6
(about 400ml / 14fl oz / 1⅔ cups)

62

1 Using a fork, carefully strip the redcurrants from their stalks. Reserve a few redcurrants for decoration and place the rest in a food processor or blender with the raspberries and icing sugar. Process until smooth.

2 Press the mixture through a fine sieve to remove all the seeds and pulp. Using a rubber spatula, transfer the purée to a small saucepan.

3 Mix the cornflour with the orange juice in a cup. Stir the mixture into the berry purée. Bring to the boil, stirring constantly, then lower the heat and simmer for 1–2 minutes until smooth and thick. Leave until cold.

4 Spoon a little of the sauce over the base of six dessert plates. Then drip the double cream from a teaspoon to make small dots around the edge of each portion, and draw a cocktail stick gently through the dots to make them into heart shapes. Scoop or spoon sorbet or poached pears into the centre of each plate. Decorate the rim of each plate with the reserved redcurrants, and add some tiny fresh flowers and leaves.

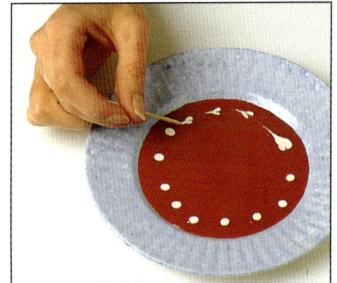

Butterscotch Sauce

INGREDIENTS

75g/3oz/6 tbsp butter
115g/4oz/³⁄4 cup soft dark brown sugar
50g/2oz/½ cup hazelnuts
175ml/6fl oz/³⁄4 cup evaporated milk

SERVES 4–6
(about 300ml/½ pint/1¼ cups)

1 Melt the butter with the sugar in a heavy-based saucepan. Bring to the boil, stirring frequently. Boil for 2 minutes, then remove from the heat and cool for 5 minutes.

2 Meanwhile, pre-heat the grill. Spread out the hazelnuts on a baking sheet and toast under the grill until golden brown. Tip on to a clean dish towel and rub briskly to remove the skins.

3 Heat the evaporated milk in a small saucepan. Gradually stir it into the sugar mixture. Cook over a low heat for 2 minutes, stirring frequently.

4 Chop the hazelnuts roughly and stir them into the sauce. Serve hot, poured over waffles or pancakes and scoops of vanilla ice cream. The sauce is also delicious with baked apples or pears.

VARIATION
Substitute pecans for the hazelnuts. Soak some sultanas in rum and add them to the sauce for an adults-only treat.

Index